THE MOON CRAWLS ON ALL FOURS

ROBIN GOW

The Moon Crawls on All Fours
Robin Gow

ISBN-13: 978-1-948712-57-6

© 2020 Robin Gow
Front Cover Image by PixelatedPeach
Front Cover Design by Weasel

Weasel Press
Lansing, MI
http://www.weaselpress.com

ALL RIGHTS RESERVED. This book contains material protected under International and Federal Copyright Laws and Treaties. Any unauthorized reprint or use of this material is prohibited. No part of this book, or use of characters in this book, may be reproduced or transmitted in any form or by any means, electronic or mechanical, including photocopying, recording, or by any information storage and retrieval system without express written permission from the author / publisher.

Contents

1

garbage island	3
on wanting to drive 5 hours to the house i grew up in	5
avenue, avenue, avenue	9
negative six degrees	11
a google search: how to []	14
individually packaged	16
strawberry window	19
this is how/	21
give me dirt	23

2

John 14:2-4	27
diorama	29
killifish	32
cuttlefish REM sleep	34
rock climbing	36
eat sugar	39
find someone	41
blue bike	44
in mom's car	46

3

on obsession	51
the phlebotomist's lover	54
glitter	56
after 3 days i give up on sleep & give in to everything else	58
how tall is	60
opportunity	62
gender	65
hydrangea	67
alone in a hotel room i don't miss home i think	70

4

Lingering	75
3 different bird calls & a car alarm	78
i want to be a tarantula	80
finally	84
this is food for ghosts	87
tuck me in	90
the capability of filling a glass	93
someone laughing	95
Self Portrait as Enough	97

The Moon Crawls on All Fours

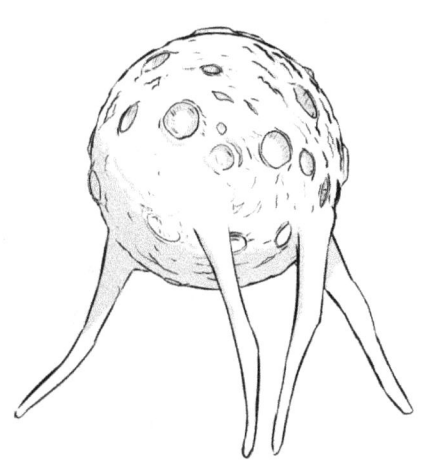

1

garbage island

i feed you chocolates
& when you leave to go home i pick
the wrappers out of
the trash, separate them &
lay them out nice like pressed petals:
foil kiss, red kitkat dress,
peppermint patty pillow case.

in the back yard i claw at the dirt
to press the wrappers into soil.
i want to grow a bed
of peanut-butter cups: their bright
milk chocolate faces blinking
towards the neon light bulb sun.

yesterday you said again
"we live on garbage island," &
all day i observed the flora
& the fauna.

with binoculars i spotted
chip bags fluttering towards
the north shore, shiny & blue,
they must have been females.

i kept a list walking
to the bus: gum slip, big gulp hat,
a bouquet of chewed straws.

i come to the one tree
on my street that cracks
the side walk: a tired oak.

4

tearing at the bark,
i want to know if the tree
is made of garbage too.
the wood comes off like
a plastic wrapper, smooth &
unnatural. inside: a trash bag liner
that i break open to find
exactly what i knew was there:

sandwich suites & shriveled
apples cores & used up lighters.
all of it, so beautiful.

i crawl inside for the rest
of the evening diving
dumpster deep in island.

what would you think of me
if you discovered me there?
would you mistake me for
a body of trash? i hope so
i hope so.

this is how you take
off my dress, tear the corner,
toss it out the car window:
let the wind do it's work.
make an island.

on wanting to drive 5 hours to the house i grew up in

i miss getting sick together
as a house.

having a small body &
swallowing grape medicine

from tiny plastic cups.

we populated the carpet
with wads of toilet paper
(never tissues)

like white carnations.

a field.

a fan blowing the petals.

windows cold
to the touch.

our hand prints.

mine bigger than yours.

i looked forward to
the ache in my body

& the fever flickering
like a mouth holding

a candle.

6

folded towels on foreheads.

me & you chewed

frozen
buttermilk waffles

on the sunken in couch.

played the static
TV channel.

there was no would outside
just us in our

sick bodies making

the house into
an eco-system.

steam from the shower
floating down the hall

& filling the upstairs.

the sun room: an angel
taking in as much

light as she could.

she asks god for
us to never get better

for us to never go apart
in healthy bodies,

heavenly bodies are often
in the process of falling apart.

there will be soup

in a pot on the stove.

italian wedding:
we get married
to the cold we
all have, make veils
from toilet paper

chicken & stars:
at night we all look out
my bed room window
& make pasta out of orion

tomato:
a whole vine in a pot.
we tell each other things
that we never do

like *please help me*

&

i'm tired

&

8
i don't want to die

&

*i love you,
thank you so much.*

picking the toilet paper
wads up from around my bed
& placing them

in the trashcan,

the flowers.
*a wedding
is over,*

i tell them.

avenue, avenue, avenue

i live on an avenue which is supposed
to have trees on both sides but
there's no trees. i say the name aloud
"Avenue, Avenue Avenue!" i say
it like i'm summoning something &
the trees start to grow from out
of the sidewalk, from in between cars:
their alarms go off so i hide inside,
i don't want anyone to know
that i did that. i look from the window,
the trees strange & varied. all
different kinds of trees. it's really
just like naming a child, naming
a street. some people probably think
over it for hours, maybe they
pace the street trying to get a feel
for what it should be called. there
was a whole neighborhood where i grew
up where all the streets were named
after books in the bible. another was
named after breeds of birds. i prefer
the birds: blue jay way, oriole avenue,
condor street, pelican circle. i don't
think a street would ever want to be called
"Leviticus," but you never know. there are
strange streets just like there are
strange children. there are children
named all sorts of things like "trout"
& "john" i grew up on a
franklin street. i could go there
& say the name aloud, a prayer, pacing
up the winding road. a boy might come,

a boy who the street was named
after or a street the boy was named after.
a ghost or otherwise he would walk
with me & i would tell him
that i don't think i will ever have
a street or children to name. maybe he would
frown or maybe he would shrug,
unsure how to comfort a grown man.
if i were in the right state of
melancholy i might ask him to be
my son. he would, of course, run away or
maybe politely refuse. either way
i would watch him walk himself
back into the "franklin" street sign,
pressing his body against the metal poll until
he disappeared. returning home
to the avenue, all the trees are
gone, cut down by the neighbors.
i will rename the avenue, but only
for myself. i'm not telling
you it either. &, maybe if years
later i get asked to name
a human i will tell them
they are named after an avenue
that no one else knew
the name of

negative six degrees

a cupped palm, a turn of hair:
i watch as the waves freeze solid

a few feet from shore. they rise
up just to hold still. a swallowed

breath. the memory of a jump
held by water. what do we do

if the water in our bodies
becomes motionless. statues;

where is medusa? a head full of
winter, a skull dripping icicle.

the ocean knows when to stop,
when to give into temperature

& write another life. this is
my chance to walk over waves.

what kind of man trusts
the ocean to stay frozen beneath

him? great tongues of blue, great
salt & salt. mermaid with me,

scales of water. a kelp curtain
clitoris where the whole atlantic

pauses before entrance. the pipes
of the house become waves too

silent & un-cracking. they tell
stories of movement & of rushing,

all the rushing & surge. a hand
in the water. a hot faucet spitting

song. i pour myself a bath but
the water lays down still. a dead

dog. getting in the bath i imagine you
finding me, not me but a peak

of water. creased & seashell-hearted
& blood turned to pipes turned

to wave. don't try to warm me.
pick me up & exhibit me. take pictures

& amble over each crest of body.
someday we will have an ocean again.

what is a lover but a frozen
ocean to try & thaw & thaw.

a dead dog. nothing to make
a handful of. in the streets there

are thousands of people becoming
statues. where do they go?

a throw from the water, we should
start calling everyone a body of salt.

i say through the ice: *it's not
our fault it's not our fault*

but it is. the house gulps.
we are warm & the light in the kitchen

is waiting with a bath drawn.

a google search: how to []

do you know that you can *make*
marshmallows?

from scratch with ingredients
in the cabinets.

i thought they were supernatural
or maybe manufactured

hold out you hands, i'm going
to mix them in your palms,

i want you sticky & syrup,
you can make marshmallows, you can

make them like cupcakes
or apple sauce, open your mouth

i want to count your marshmallows
i mean teeth, you have

to be careful or you'll grow
marshmallows all from

your gums: gelatin, sugar,
corn syrup, sugar, cold water.

what if we're already marshmallow?
let's mix inside your mouth,

open, lift me in. the swell
of a hot marshmallow, your tongue

gone white with worry. i promise
this is all temporary, nothing

marshmallow lasts very long.
there's the microwave to make

swell of that. your teeth will
dissolve, yes, but they will be

sweet. they will be homemade
& your will know every single

speck of sugar inside. let's
count them, i'll line them

up on your taste bugs: pink
stippling. a farm. doesn't everyone

want to use their mouth
as a bowl full of hot? a bowl

full of fingers & teeth?
one big huge marshmallow all

stuck under my fingernails.
that's you. that's loving someone

all day all night all mixing.
a campfire on your palette.

a marshmallow, just one
between us, swelling huge.

individually packaged

everything's wrapped up
around here, the cellophane
round the dead trees,
standing bent
as dried sea horses,
try to find the corner
to undo them,
picking with my nails.

then of course there's
the tupperware with whole
houses instead. i approach
but there's no way i could
pry off the clear red lid
on my own,
is this where you live?
behind a dull wall.
does it keep you all fresh?

do your parents tell
your to lay down on
press & seal: roll you up.
you make a crinkling body.
i but you smell like
cilantro & lemongrass.
you stay young.

outside someone comes
by each day to wrap birds
in foil, twisting up each
in the shape of swans.
they perch all across

the yard, occasionally
rustling & i say
ssh ssh
hold still, you'll spoil.

TEAR HERE
says a cloud. i reach for
the plastic corner, pinch
between fingers. i think
for a second that maybe
i shouldn't. that maybe
i'll ruin everything if i open
this all up.

i think of you wrapped up
in bed & your parents in their
own separate tupperwares,
everything so crisp.
i will eat you someday,
i mutter.

i pull the corner
& the sky lets out a sigh,
like taking off pants
like spilling a glass
of orange juice that wanted
to topple over all along.

all the packaging holding
in a May mouthful of
wanting behind the seal.

i know this means
we'll go bad. we'll ripen & rot

terribly soon.
a kind of organic panic.
i want to look at
your house from far away.
to see it contort:
an apple core
a collapsing swan
a drying sea horse.

strawberry window

voice all thumb print
on the open window:
outside someone is singing
& their voice comes in smooth
like a hard caramel.
sweet saliva dew. i want
to crawl into that mouth
& feel each note hum through me.
i'll be her handful of harpsichord.
i'll be her plastic kuzoo.
this winter's gone strawberry
with bouts of mud.
i reach my arm out, hoping
to clutch a fragment
of that ribbon-ing melody
but instead catch
a blue robin's egg
as it drops from a bare tree.
cold planet pluto, a melting
piece of hail with a glass bird
inside. the trees,
like adam & eve, realize
on this strange
night that they aren't wearing
any leaves. they reach for
shirt. i give them away
each one button at a time,
one for you
one for you
& this is not enough
so the one takes
my floral print button-up shirt

& the other takes me teal pants,
draping the garment over a branch.
they weep, knowing that they're
still so naked. they don't
pay attention like i do
as i hear the singing
getting farther away.
what song is that?
i ask again & again
but there's only me
& the sobbing oaks &
the melting egg still dripping
in my palm. i could follow
the voice, i know,
but that would ruin
the mystery of it. i crawl back
in through the open window
& lay on my own voice,
the floor of my office
where the egg turns
completely into liquid
& the glass bird is too
small to speak. i let
the singing fade out into
another laugh of wind.
what song was that?
what song?
& how would it feel
inside that mouth, under
a warm wet tongue
as the tune trickled
& clothed me.

this is how/

i cut/ myself
with a spoon/ the edge dipped
into wrist/ where everyone starts/
im ice cream/ im sherbet/ pink
& i eat/
& there's flavor/
like cut finger nails / & metal.
a chewing gum/ named
"aluminum." spoonful
by spoonful/ behind
a locked door/ where
i like to eat/ everything/
& there's nothing left/
for you. i want someone/
to love me/ so hard that
i don't come back/ here
& stare / at the sharp hems
of spoons. oh dixie cup/
i devour/ alone so /
you don't/ get to see/
what face i make/ with each
cool slip/ of silver
into skin/ pint after pint/
i cut/ myself/
with spoons/
delicious/ melt/
a whole drawer/ of options
for ways to/ make
this body/ i want to/
love/ someone /
who lives like
i do/ spoons/

in backpacks/ lodged
in their bones/ surgical
tools/ a memory
of a boy holding/
a spoon/ over my/ mouth
like a bowl/
don't/ stir/ me

give me dirt

you blew on my face till
all the hairs of my dandelion beard
came flying off: each parachute seed
planting himself in the dry grass lawn:
a crop of small boys growing: gold weed boys:
saw-tooth leaf boys: boasting about
their fathers: each saying: *mine is bigger*:
mine is bigger: i don't tell them
i'm all their fathers because: i like to
see them arguing: builds character:
they think it might: make them taller:
they imagine turning: from weed to tree:
that's not how this works: they look:
at each others: dress shoes in the soil:
each lace's leather roots: dug into earth:
i remember pulling weeds out from the church
garden by their necks: my own father's:
green garden gloves: the feet of each weed
dangling as we ripped them from
beneath a bush: of lamb's ear: pick
one man from the whole bunch: how many:
children's feet: baby shoes as planters:
i could fill every inch of the house: with
tiny: match box: beds: for all the small men:
all my fault for letting hair: crop up
on my face: where all weeds come from:
you don't have to know about this: i tell myself:
as i get on my knees: in front of: all the men:
they don't recognize me: they come over:
touch my smooth bare face: i don't tell
them: *this is where you came from*:
but maybe they know: i tell them i have

no home for them: their shoes get bigger:
the size of my dad's shoes: great size 13s:
pushing up grass: dirt: calm down men: calm:
i don't have enough: soil in my chest:
for all those shoes: for all the learning
how to tie a tie: for all the yellow clamor:
pick the seeds off strawberries: to feed them:
i don't tell you: i'd be embarrassed: plus i like
when you blow: all the hair off my face: you don't need to know:
i'm full of growing: i try to keep the seeds inside: under tongue:
in freckle: in skin: each screaming: father: father: father: give me dirt

2

John 14:2-4

what we didn't know was that heaven would be lonely
& how much we'd miss wanting things.
a plate with a scoop of whipped cream,
four of us huddled in the center,
barefoot & asking each other
if anyone has seen an angel.
we don't talk to each other because
heaven meet every need we could ever have.
we're grouped together because we
all like the same temperature & humidity.
none of us remember where we're from
but i remember that when i had a body
i used to burn my mouth on hot french fries
& now when i eat french fries i never
burn my mouth,
i can't, it's impossible.
everything here is smooth
even the stubble on my face
like a forehead of a rabbit.
sometimes the plate grows
green vines all around
& i follow them
hoping they might lead me away
from here to a different heaven.
when i first got here i thought
i loved the others more
than anything but
it is tiresome to love everything
about other entities,
we have nothing to talk about
we nod to each other
& we ask each other's names

even though we know
none of us have them.
i once wanted to be disobedient
& ate the green vines by the handful
but they turned to licorice
when they touched my mouth.
i wish i was a terrible human
in the bone life because
now i'm terrible in heaven
& i have no where to go.
i crouch alone & pretend
it's afternoon,
which i remember as being
like the sky dropped
a spoonful of honey
on herself.
i sit alone,
walk on all fours out of curiosity
& occasionally i love the loneliness
how everything is what i want
& what i want only, the unbridled
selfishness of it all.
i scan the sky for angels
& remember insects with with colorful wings.
the vines grow
& i lay down on them,
overhearing two of the bodies in the distance
ask each other
what is your name?

diorama

with the same impulse
that Noah built a great wooden
arc i've started making
a diorama of a one-room school house
this is where i will move to
if i get too small for
the real world, i imagine
waking up one day as tall
as a pen. i collect coins
& pine cones,
setting up match boxes
for desks & a chalk board
where i'll write the date
desks in rows as if
they were planted
by a farmer. desks turning
into plants, tomato vines
& soybeans, there were
all sorts of school houses
floating in the midst
of the fields where i grew
up & i wanted to crawl
in through the windows
& live there, become
a nice match box,
listen to the laughter
of wind playing tag
in tall corn,
when my house floods
over i will have this
diorama,
all the detail,

the care it takes to
make everything smaller,
have you ever tried
to build a model?
i have, i left them all unfinished
on a table upstairs,
a half-painted titanic
& a biplane with one wing,
maybe i'll put them
in the diorama too,
just for safe keeping,
what i haven't decide yet
is what people will belong
inside, taking handfuls
of ants to make the school children,
crawling on the shoe box walls,
on their desks, what misbehavior,
did god do this? feel like this
about his animals? all over
the place, i will be
a pen, tall & full of blue ink,
all this life i'll write
on the classroom walls,
i'll look out the window
& see the seasons swimming past
each other, summer with
its six legs, autumn:
the shell of a peanut,
winter: a rolling blueberry,
spring: pink eraser
i take the school house
& i dump it in the lawn
to start over, i need
it to be perfect,

i ask the ants
what they'll want
to be when they grow up,
but they just scatter,
i wonder about
the real school houses
if anyone ever crawls
in through the windows
lays on the cool floor,
listens to the seasons whirl

killifish

feed me baby spoon swallows
of dioxin/ PCB
jars in my throat
i'm here to talk to
the killifish
to open all my fingers
& have them swim between
knots of yellow
glinting scales
mouthful of minnow
the gulf of my blood where
they dump all the bad stories
killifish have evolved
to survive the bay's deadly toxins
their deformed hearts
like salted strawberries
bodies all see-through
in the eggs
i ask to be be see-through
& soft like that
let the chemicals
play with my genomes
i want to mutate
with them
thrive in their strangeness
this is the only option left
as far as i can tell
so i talk to them
i nestle in their muck
the ocean
all yellow with hand lotion
plastic bottles float

by & the killifish say
someday we will gnash plastic too
someday there will be
nothing we can't turn into body
clumps of their vein blue eyes
never blink
stare louder
i cup my hands to catch
killifish, open to
let them dart away
they shriek with evolution
they call me
drowning monkey
i cut gills in my neck
to prove them wrong
i say
i'm one of you
i'm one of you

cuttlefish REM sleep

fill body with invisible color
oh glory grey scale, turn
inside out red & get black
the cuttlefish changes textures
& shades but only sees in black/white
i'm going to tell her about
all of the prisms ringing
on her skin, outstretch
my arms till i have only
three of them, like her, the blue
water not blue but clear
thick with sound waves
thick with animal skins
who wouldn't want to know
what it's like to sleep in the body
of each fish & shark
& octopus & cuttlefish?
i'm here chewing mollusk shells
till all the bones
inside me fuse like hers,
the one long bone inside
the cuttlefish often washes
up on shore, used to sharpen
knives, i'll pull mine
out through my mouth &
use it to sharpen the paring
knives in my mother's kitchen,
i'll show her my new beak
& my new undulating eyes,
turned tie dye as i sleep
in the sink with the dishes,
when cuttlefish enter REM sleep

they pulse with rainbow waves
& patterns flickering across
their skin,
watercolor projector screen skin
maybe inside
they can know their colors,
invent new words for
red & purple & orange, maybe
naming them after other cuttlefish
who they once enjoyed
the company of
in the sink i think how
i would name yellow after you
& purple after my mother
& maybe name red after myself
i stand there, on
a sandy beach, picking
cuttlefish bones off the shore
& slipping them into a backpack
at home i'll hide them
in case i need to sharpen
a knife or re-teach hardness
to my bones,
swallowing one
all my skin turning grey
then the walls of the house
& you even though you're
far away
i wanted this
for us

rock climbing

the floor is dissolving
one foot print
at a time, first the hardwood
then the gnarled living room carpet &
slick bathroom tiles
i keep thinking of our childhood games
of "red hot lava" climbing
on furniture to escape the invisible
calamity waiting for us on the floor
of our parent's house
lava in the carpet, lava between
the legs of the round kitchen table
lava swallowing & burning the TV
when i was in 5th grade you
had a birthday party
at the rock climbing
place & you said you were practicing
for when the bottom eventually falls out from the world
how did you know all the way back then?
i didn't believe you
the next day
my arms tingled like they'd been squeezed all night
feeling every muscle i raised
each limb slowly,
pretending to pluck
my ceiling light down, a ripe white fruit
you snuck in from your room to lay
next to me & we compared muscle shapes
you said you wanted to nail
rock climbing rocks to all the walls
of the house & i imagined climbing
everywhere with the lava licking

at our shoes
all night i'm nailing rocks
to all the walls
each foot step counts
because where it was will
then disappear as lift my foot
i wonder if this is happening where
you are too,
i haven't seen you
in months & i hope your voice
sounds the same,
where is the whole floor
of the world going?
i imagine each foot print building
a new planet
house by house
maybe each step the people there make
adds ground instead
of taking it away
you of all people will be okay though,
i remember watching you
at the old rock climbing place from below,
you didn't need the black harness
you moved, a spider far above
all the other kids
gripping stone after stone
after stone,
i hang onto the wall,
planting rocks of all different colors
all the way to the front door
where i hold on & wait
i'm so scared you will come
& open the door just
to fall in

i practice saying
"the floor is hot lava"
so that you won't
tumble away
as your take
your first step inside

eat sugar

the moon crawls
on all fours in through
the window after watching me
all night, great white eye with
the pupil gone wandering in the dirt
as an ant. hungry moon, i feed it
spoonfuls of sugar in the kitchen,
sand-like white piles, i consider each
grain a different word i would have said
if the moon was someone i loved or if the moon
knew anything about how much glow a human body
can have. i want to peel the moon open to look at it's
organs. what kind of organs do moons have? maybe just
the same as ours. there might be houses somewhere
with no windows. the moon grows more legs
the longer it stays on earth, unspooling,
a knot of centipedes, i pour sugar
on the floor because the moon
is impatient, i open the fridge,
get eggs to throw at the moon
who runs, hiding beneath
the sofa, turning into
an egg itself, do you know
that if you spin an egg
on the counter you can tell
if it's cooked or not? if it spins
perfectly it's cooked, if it wobbles it's
raw, the moon wobbles, is a raw egg, i don't have
time to cook the moon, i step outside
in the cold March night, which is supposed
to be spring but fucking isn't,
where i throw the egg at the sky

hoping it will go back up there
but instead it splats against
a neighbor's window
so, i run back to inside,
peer out my own window,
through the blinds to see
the moon sitting up there again,
this time as a hand mirror,
reflecting just my own
face back at me,
close up. i go back
to the kitchen
spin eggs on the counter,
eat sugar.

find someone

the carnival sprawls,
first just a block,
outside my house with a few
booths: a dart game, a ferris wheel,
a tilt-a-whirl,
now every street i know, all
of them blocked off,
we have cars but no one uses
them anymore
we go to the carnival
& i forget just
where i lost you in the midst of blink
& laughter but i count the 3 tickets
in my pocket saying 1, 2, 3
1, 2, 3 as if that might summon you
from out of the whirl of color
& metal, last summer
i would pass by the carnivals
& say to myself that i should
go back, that i should
find someone to go to the carnival with
but i never did &
i now they've come for me
or at least that what i think,
maybe it's something else entirely
a new plan for the city,
every street full of amusements
full of people i don't recognize,
i don't know anyone at the carnival
they're converting all the apartments
into fun houses, men with gloves
installing mirrors on all our walls

i wonder if i pace the halls
if i might find you in the glass
pull you free & we can go
to the carnival together,
i could show you my favorite ride
or we can get away, though
i don't know where we would go
or if i want to leave anymore
i miss those nights where
i was so in love with you
there was no where else
we could go but my room
tracing each other's
bodies, laying up against the wall,
taking a pen & leaving our
outlines there, i spent a
ticket to get inside my own house
& there's glass where we used
to sleep together,
i press hand prints there
i have 2 tickets & i'm saving
them for us,
so much carnival
so much carnival all over,
ringing in my teeth
my teeth also turned
to mirrors,
i hope wherever you
are that you ended up
in a beautiful patch
of carnival & that you remember me
& that you eat fried dough
with powdered sugar &
the glittering noise of machine

reminds you i exist,
maybe you'll even think
about my outline on
the bed room wall &
i'll say outside
& will go inside the fun house
& stay there, watching
our reflections as they
move closer to each other
touch skin
carnival churning
outside

blue bike

bicycles with no riders
cluster together in packs
rushing through down my street
at 11pm making squawking goose sounds
a flock of them
searching looking for others
i pear glance out the window
to watch view them
all different types:
tricycles
ones wearing with training wheels
old rusted face flat tire bikes
beautiful white wall tire pastel pink ones
their owners have to miss need them
i think remember my own bike
with the shiny blue body
and bell we fixed screwed to handlebars
the noise chirp it made
as i rushed road through alleyways in town
& back up to my gravel driveway
i wonder ponder if my blue bike
ran away escaped with a pack of bikes
like the one that comes through
my street at night
i check scan the pack closer
with the idea i might see my old blue bike
that i might convince persuade
the bike to come home
& sit lay in my living room
while i tell speak stories to the bike
about how much i loved adored it
all those years

changing shifting gears
to make it up the big hill by
the playground
laying resting the bike
down in the grass while
i played wallball against on
the brick back of the high school building
i imagine think it's contagious
the bikes tell teach each other
one by one
that they can move with no rider
and soon enough they're following going
with the group
all the bikes laughing chortling
in the street
my street each night around 11
and everyone just hears mistakes
them for geese

in mom's car

the floor of
the station wagon collected us:
white grease-stained fast food bags
handfuls of sand
smashed pine cones.
held our relics close
and asked us to bring more,
opening all doors
the trunk gaping mouth
seats giving into soil.
together on long car trips
trees would have time enough to
sprout tall
the car imagining a world
for us
folding us deeper inside
her blue metal skull
the doors miles away,
did the car plan to keep us?
my brother and i,
meandering in
different forests and deserts
losing a bracelet
a ring
a kazoo a clementine
we ambled
seat belts slung over our shoulders,
sometimes, calling out
each other's names
just to hear how deep the echo would go.
forgetting this was our mom's car,
that, somewhere,

she was holding
a steering wheel like a sun hat.
did she wander too?
barefoot maybe did she
forget that she had children?
we never talked about it
when we found our ways out
back to the doors
brushing dirt off legs
from the jungles
and prairies the car build
from our own discharged items
we were going somewhere
there was somewhere outside
the car
i wonder though, if, sometimes,
she took long rides alone.
if on those rides
mom might have wanted to stay there
bringing sandwich wrappers to her car
like offerings
asking to go away somewhere
with a faint breeze,
wearing the steering wheel on her head
as a sunhat.

3

on obsession

i have recently discovered
the powering of slamming doors.

maybe i had always known,
but yesterday it started by accident,

just a desire to shut, a thrust,
the swing behind me,

the rattle of the hinge like
clenched teeth, the slap of

wood against the frame, the front
door & its gold knob nose

aching because of me. after
that i had a need to do it more.

you have to understand this
isn't out of anger, this is a way

of existing. have you slammed
a door lately? i do it whenever

i have the chance. in & out
of my bedroom, the click,

a mouth with the teeth
all fallen out. i collect

molars off the hard wood floor
& slip them back into the frame.

i slam my mouth like a door,
my nose gone golden.

freshman year of college
i had a roommate who would

shut the door loud again
& again late into the night.

i thought she was insane,
in the dark i pushed my eyes

shut as she threw the door,
the thick heavy door, banging our

box of a room. i understand her
now, i think. i want to ask her

what it felt like to stand
outside in the dorm room hall

pushing the door again & again.
had she been angry? had she just

needed to feel real? i understand
i do. i wish she would had

shown me then so i could
get it out of my system young.

i can't stop now.
i try to find a new door each day,

ambling up to strangers houses
& asking politely if i can open

& shut their front door.
each type of wood, each house

has a different pleasing sound.
i lay in bed shutting my mouth

like my roommate once shut that door.
again & again, i collect

the teeth from my pillow
& put them back in.

the phlebotomist's lover

as he puts the rubber band around my forearm

i explain that i sometimes faint

when i have my blood drawn & by sometimes i mean

that once i went with my mom in 8th grade &
the nurse tried to tell me that she once took
Jerry Seinfeld's blood & i didn't know who that was.
i felt as if i were crawling, hands & knees
through a tunnel & then i woke up
to the coral green waiting room.

as he puts the rubber band around my forearm

i want to ask him what his lover thinks of this,

if he or she or they know that each day

he takes the cool sharp needle, tells

boys like me to "talk to him" & to

"tell me something about yourself."

i imagine telling him that i associate needles
with family. that each time i have my blood drawn
i see all of the standing in the corner
of the sterile white room & i mean all of them,
i mean aunts & grandmom & brothers & mom & dad,
all of them watching me let this man plunge
the needle deep into my arm, blood filling his

vials quickly, a quick gush & nothing more.

as he takes the rubber man away from around my forearm

i try to remember what i told him in that moment

& i think i said that i have a little brother who

is 6 years old (which is a lie, he's 10)
& that he misses me while i'm at college which
is also probably a lie because he doesn't
know me any different, i've always been in school.

as he takes the rubber man away from around my forearm

i want to as him if it's really over

if all we were was an exchange of blood, if

at night he lays next to his lover & tells

them about all the bodies he entered,

holding up his fingers to count them,
maybe stopping as he remembers me. maybe
he skips me because what we had was too alive
to have just been 8 vials of blood.
does he keep one & tell no one?

glitter
-After CA Conrad

was it this year or the last
when all my blood turned to glitter?
standing at the bathroom sink
i watched quietly the glint
of each reflecting speck
as it trickled from a nick
in my thumb. i imagined
what i would look like
with all my skin shed off,
a crowded constellation
of a body.
i tell everyone i can find
that there's no such thing
as blood, at least not anymore.
does that count as a prophecy?
maybe not. i roll up my pant leg
to show the shimmering scab
on my knee & i say
look i have proof.
most people who pass are
confused, they quicken
their step as i add
you have it too
you have it too.
i think a lot about how
salt turns a slug inside out
& what ingredient that
is for humans. i'd like
to lay down in it, pour
glitter, gush glitter,
stain the side walk

with all my glitter for
someone else to clean up.
an inside out human, would
anyone recognize me or
would a gust of wind work fast to scatter:
colorful ashes,
metallic hands clapping at light.
until then i sneak into
the kitchen. dull flicker
of dusk. a pairing knife.
a cereal bowl. i make a small
basin of glitter from
an incision in my side,
yes i go biblical but i bet
jesus wasn't full of
glitter like us.

after 3 days i give up on sleep & give in to everything else

an 8 is a 3 with it's
mouth all closed & i laid
awake thinking of how it feels
to put your thumb on the not-sharp
side of the knife.
i peel myself up, some kind
of rind fruit, my stuff
all orange & sweet
cantaloupe or tangerine:
with necks like puckered eyes.
somewhere my mom was snoring
& my dad compared the noise
to a chain saw. it cut holes
in the drywall.
it gnawed a silhouette
of everyone, haunting
a house by nightlights,
dad & his living ghost.
do i talk in my sleep?
i might & if i do it's
not me but a string
of previous selves desperate
for a mouth to make
promises with.
listen to them & write
them down, this
is where the knife
comes in again:
cut the language
into the bed post
or the wall. no i don't
have a bedpost. i have
a twin

sized bed & most days
its size feels coffin like,
i hope they don't bury
me with you, there's
not enough room &
if i'm going to
be an 8 i'd like to
have room for decorations.
a bowl for a cave fish,
still hearing her snores
under the earth
i ask someone if it's
just an earth quake.
no answer just the house
crinkling & reptilian,
metal-scaled & shrugging
off a playground insult
making its way through
the pipes.
i ask the house
if it will dig
the hole for me,
not too deep, not six feet
i need to be able to crawl
out if i change my mind.
a gust of wind rattles us.
i put my thumb to the back
of a knife, stand there
by the sink just caressing,
ignoring the other side.
i open my mouth to talk
with both of my mouths:
one to laugh &
one to ask for silence
& sleep.

how tall is

i walk on dark stilts
in the parking lot, back & forth
what kind of bird?
my guillotine shadows saunter
removing the heads of plastic bag ghosts,
slicing parking spaces
like pound cake.

the top shelf is not
all that far away now &
then i won't have to ask you
to stretch your talons up
to pull another bird's nest down
by the neck

each day i add another foot
to my new legs, teach
myself how to stumble
taller & taller, as high as
the water tower, mouth full
of mouth:
a water balloon tongue

when the cars scream their horns
i shout back, dead cranes
calling out with both of
our beaks, we have
a conversation about
the sadness of driving
in new york with the rain spitting
to remind us how unclean
we still feel

you wouldn't recognize me
so elevation.
head bumped on the hot-faced moon,
is this how tall is a man?

i slow dance the lamps
in the parking lot, call
them sweet names like "dearest"
& "doll"
each almost as tall
as me

a waltz sound crawls
on all fours from the grates
so i sway alone, circling
the carcass of my car
like a condor, soft
green meat of
a passenger seat

i call out again
to no horn in particular,
it's loon & lonely
out here

add another foot,
steady myself

at least
i'm tall now

opportunity

my battery is low &
it is getting dark

who did the mars rover imagine
in his last moments crossing

the scabbed ground? the god
of war lived round & copper

beneath him. we should pray
him into heaven like we do

each year for my aunt joan.
15 years ago when he first landed

she was still alive & dyed
her hair the same color as his rocks.

his sphere-attic world
laughing under his feet, she held

the counter to make her way
through the kitchen. i see

myself at 15 walking mars:
a girl in a purple halter dress

& blue hair, perched
on a precipice looking over

the relics of a martian sea.
she draws starfish in the pie-crust

ground before the darkness
encroaches on all sides. taste

of dying sits in the back of her throat
like chewing aluminum foil.

what angels does she meet?
what other gods did our mars rover know?

building shrines in his machinery,
a solitary worship, his altar of red giants,

each a candle lit by the bold &
stubborn death of a star. he sings

to himself like i do, like
my aunt joan did, even as she was dying,

her voice leaving her body
as a ribbon into the ceiling fan,

even farther above the rover hummed.
did he pretend that he had parents?

a normal life? high school years?
a first love far far below?

the 15 year old me up there buckles
& falls like the trunk of a tree.

my aunt took years. her gaze always
drifting farther & farther above our

heads as she forgot us more each day.
did she know the rover somehow?

did they talk? did she tell them
her life stories as they left her.

i know he listened, kept those stories,
repeated the details to himself for comfort:

a green wave on the jersey beach,
two white shell-shaped clip-on earrings.

the rover's eyes go dark slowly,
the thinning of throat, he hears

the transmission commanders as they call
for him, all his fathers,

hears Billie Holiday singing
"I'll be seeing you

In all the old familiar places,"
thinks of everyone else who

died too young & says to himself
"what good company i am in."

gender

avocados change their
sex every day:
female by day
male by night.
more avocado trees.
plant them in my hair
plant them in sidewalk cracks
and the gaps in my teeth.
i want so many avocado trees
to duck under, the fruit
swelling like fat green tears drops,
plopping down on my body,
leaving bruises in the shape
of perfect circles,
polka-dots or bulls-eyes
or third eyes.
i'll tell them it's okay,
that there are humans
who experience the same
gender tumbling.
i peel a fruit
put the pit in my mouth
to suck on
it's sensual,
big round heavy seed
spit in the dirt.
i'll show the trees my nail polish
i'll show the trees the scars
where my breasts used to be
they will understand then
what sex means,
the pollen all night

all night
shouting pollen at
the earth, how dare the pollen
so yellow
sticky on my hands.
oh avocado trees
make a female of me by day
so that i can make
fruit like yours,
blooming from my hair
pump ripe green,
i pluck them to fill
a bowl on the counter
my avocado,
finger nails
dig into the tough skin
soft innards,
muted color texture
god of avocados
save the pits

hydrangea

he puts his nose to my ear
smells the April in me,
the May making purple
pink blue
i tell him that he's
caught me
get the trow
distrust the science
of brains
my family grown hydrangeas
in our skulls
we eat dirt for the roots
drink water but never too much
drowned so many
good flowers that way
water gushing from
noses water making
mush soil
count the petals
all afternoon
assigned female at birth
assigned fragrance at birth
assigned floral at birth
we knew grandmom
was gone when she started
smelling like wet leaves
blue roots crawling under
her hands
i see mine there too
only they're not
as angry yet
he's not the first

boy to notice
doesn't ask
just stares
into my open mouth
admires the garden
plans a bench behind
my eyes so he can
watch my life unfold
stained glass iris
he doesn't like
girls which is good
because i'm not a girl
which is good because
his trow is covered
in dirt
which is good because
i want him
to dig
i lower my head like
i'm going to be
blessed or knighted
my mother told me
that my great great
grandmother planted
the first hydrangea
i curse her softly
why me
he smells like hot rain
scoops the earth
he loves it
i say
deeper
he says
petals

i say
ignore them
he says
how could i?

alone in a hotel room i don't miss home i think

i think of what all i could fit inside
the tiny hotel fridge
two rows of bottles clink against each other
when i tug on the door
rain turns to glass
glass to rain
smaller versions of wine bottles
each too small to climb inside
i could fit maybe four books
inside the hotel fridge
if i laid the books sideways
or maybe all the clothing
from my suite case
all folded up like i never do
because i hate folding
& i hate packing
i prefer to crumple t-shirts & pants
each like a carnation
pressed under textbooks
it makes traveling feel less real
like a sleepover
a commitment to going home
& i am going home just not now
open the door of the fridge again
a cold mouth full of glass
i take out all the drinks
& line them up on the soft floor
my guests
a little parade
spread them out so they don't touch
they make a wall
they hold hands without having hands

i could empty them each
in the clean white sink
just to see the pouring
just to have an empty fridge
to climb into
i wonder if it could lead somewhere
putting my whole head inside
the whirl of refrigeration
blue taste
dull white glow
i imagine the people who clean rooms coming
to ready my room for the next guest &
finding the fridge door open
getting on their knees to peer inside
& finding no one
just a small tunnel in the fridge
where i would sit on the other side
in a room full of television screens
playing videos of everyone
who ever stayed in the same hotel room
not just images of them living in the room
but their whole lives
pressing hands to windows
climbing inside fridges
the room still cold
the walls still fridge white
& in the distance
the ever present gentle sound
of bottle clinking against bottle
fingers clinking against fingers
taking off my clothing
& stepping on my shirt & pants like carnations
but i don't go inside
not tonight

i put all the bottles back
on my knees
they clink as i set them in their rows
lay out on the bed
try to imagine the other people's bodies
who've laid there
night after night

4

Lingering

My feet touch the cold sidewalk
as I take out one bag
of trash to the curb.

No one else is out there
but me and my feet,
and there is a light,
hesitant rain that
reminds me of amphibians.

I want to find toads
on my porch but I haven't seen on
since moving to Long Island.

My bare feet want to walk
the whole street,
a pair of toads,
soft as their white underbellies.

I wonder how many feet
there are living around here,
and if anyone else ever
thinks about the feel of cool sidewalk
on a night in April or otherwise.

I'm imagining everyone
stepping out and standing still
just for a second,
barefoot, looking around
at their street
in the shimmery mist
slick on stone sidewalk and asphalt

that hold up our houses.

Standing over the pile of trash,
I try to make out the shapes all inside
and I find a paper plate
folded in half.

There is no moon,
so I decide that the moon
is the paper plate hidden
under the plastic skin
of the trash bag.

I think about what
my feet might feel like
ambling on the surface
of the moon, if it might
feel chalky and warm,
and, maybe, its glow
feels on the skin
like wanting to speak.

I want to tell someone about this,
but it's late,
and I should go inside.

But it's late
and I should remove my feet
from the ground,
fold them in blankets,
dark and quiet,
tell them to hold their breath,
and no be so dreamy
when we're trying to inside.

Each body part, then, seems
like an argument for lingering,
for asking sensation
what it means for the whole,
for asking if everything
can be felt underneath us,
or if there are objects
we have to know less intimately.

Inside, I take a paper plate
and stand on it.
It sticks to my toes and heel.
The plate feels loose and shifting,
un-sturdy as I would assume
that moon too might feel.

3 different bird calls & a car alarm

pours a bag of feathers
all over me
the sun & the whole thrum
awake without me
i turn over like a sausage
in a skillet,
like the ones mom made
every morning
a browning edge &
grease softly folding
alive under skin
the spatter & crackle of heat
i ask the brightness
to keep on going out there
to reflect off hoods of cars
to kick up dirt
& scoop the voices
of the birds nesting in the garage
make lives out of them
send the birds to college
& miss them when they move away
i am a red glow & i thought
for a moment i was waking up
in my parents big queen sized bed
with the black ceiling fan overhead,
a spider to twirl
they had a painting of two rock fish
on the wall above them
i looked to see if it was there
& there is someone awake
in the ceiling
maybe just a pair of feet

maybe there's only upstairs
& no sky
just white drywall
& flickers of dreams
where we were in disney world
i think only
you all had forgotten
each other
besides me
i remembered &
i tried to remind each
family member
of sometime we were up
too early together
there are so few people
who see us wake up
what do i lose when
someone sees me, if they
watch me decide when to
pull myself up?
this might be why lovers
have to share beds
to watch the other emerge
from a warm murk
blink & shut eyes
the bag of feathers poured
over head
the rolling of bodies
in a skillet
the whole family
all turkey sausage links
i'm full of grease today
i ask the birds to come in
& sit with me

i want to be a tarantula

you tell me you've been watching videos
of tarantulas molting.
so, when i'm alone later that night
i find one to watch.
i cup the iPhone screen in my hands,
moving it away from my body,
as if it were a tarantula.
unable to look away,
the spider crawls out of itself,
like a glove emerging from
another glove,
soul crawling on eight legs
out of its last body.
is it a new animal?
i wonder if maybe the molted
tarantula has vague memories
of the other body's life,
but, never quite remembers
having been a smaller creature.
the other body:
crumpled like a coat
in the corner.
i imagine a row
of all the tarantula's skins
hung up in a closet,
the tarantula perusing
them, & forgetting that
those had been him.
i watch the video again,
over & over, fast forwarding
to the part where the spider
makes it's last tug

& is free from the old husk,
the husk falling back,
the new body more vibrant,
orange bright fur around
each knee,
deeper black body.
i have the urge to touch
the tarantula, i want to know
if its new body is damp,
if it's slick from bursting
out of the first.
there must be a human equivalent
to all of this.
i sit on the hard wood floor
of my room
& inspect my skin
for points where i might
fissure, where another
boy might come out of me,
maybe taller this time,
maybe with glowing skin
& straighter teeth
& bigger hands.
i open my closet,
find all the hangers
hold tarantula skins,
a range of sizes.
the smallest ones
are crumbly from age
so i put my arms into
a middle-sized one, get down
on the floor & try to
amble like i saw the spiders
do in the videos.

i pause & recreate how
they molt, slowly & deliberately
rising from the skin
heaving forward,
i worry about being caught
in the act,
like masturbating but
somehow more personal, more intimate,
i worry about you seeing me
like this,
a creature with eight legs
on the ground
eight legs into two
i molt from tarantula
to human & i cry
because it felt almost real,
like i was coming out
of my skin & into a new one,
like the body i would
stand up in would
be glistening & vibrant.
i leave the skin tossed
on the floor & watch more
videos of tarantulas molting,
rewinding, trying to see
what it is they feel that moment
they step out,
regret? fear?
whatever happens there,
i think it is something
that i can't have.
i make peace with that,
ask the tarantula to come
crawl out of the screen,

tell me what its
new life will be.

finally

cars with their headlights off
at night, delete themselves.

ghost vehicles, passing between
other cars, made of cold air.

dislodged from everything,
slowly becoming part of the backdrop,

i imagine them sinking into
the asphalt, like descending a

staircase. i consider turning
my car's headlights off

to see what happens, to see
if maybe that slight adjustment

could alter everything.
finally invisible, finally flying,

only an underground kind of flight
below the street like the movement

of the subway, the way you can
sometimes look down at a metal grate

in the sidewalk & feel how close
how close the shuttering is.

i walk into the basement
without trying to turn on the light,

wading into the dark,
it has a kind of thickness like

if i held up a spoon i could
scoop the black & eat it,

a coarse jelly. i imagine
the basement full of cars

with their headlights off, all
of them racing towards me,

only i won't see them because
i'm stubborn & i won't turn

the light on, just a white switch
a simple click but i want that

lingering, treading absence,
i want that darkness down there

to envelop me, keep me safe,
few of us will admit that

we don't always want to know the truth,
that we turn off the headlights

of our cars & think of being invisible
for a few seconds,

envision collision, smack of metal
bodies into each other, one body

unseen, reaching the floor of
the basement, feeling for the switch

& finally throwing light into
the room, the fear there.

this is food for ghosts

do you ever remember things
that didn't happen?

there's a yellow room
& she's opening a sugar packet
onto my tongue, a little mountain
built there, melting
sweet sand. she opens
a sugar pack into her mouth
then, too,
& somehow we kiss,
which makes me think
of hummingbird throats full of nectar.

a window's open, white
curtain, blue curtain,
a wind blowing papers off
a desk, all scattered, i'm stepping
on top of them.

i take all the lunch meat
out of the fridge, separate
salami & bologna & ham
onto plates. she's there
again & she folds the meats
like blankets. i tell her
the food is for the ghosts
in our house & she eats
a piece & says "good then,
it's for me."

we saw a hummingbird

in the church garden,
no, no i didn't, *she* saw
a humming bird in the church
garden, & i was so jealous
i drew sketches of hummingbirds
on the papers scattered on
the floor blown free
by the open window
that no one opened,
that might not have
been open.

she has a swimming pool
& we sneak out in the middle of
the night & fill it with sugar,
packets meticulously opened
one at a time, the music
of tearing paper. she jumps
in while i work, floating
on her back, mouth puckering
like a catfish to suck in sugar.
i ask to get in & she says "no"
she says that i'm making
this up because i am,
i don't want a non-made-up memory.

i make a sugar bowl
of my head, carve out the brains,
the soft pinkness & pour white sugar all in.
my head, a swimming pool.
i hang curtains from my eyelids
so they can blow open white blue.
i invite the humming birds,
draw them on the palms of my hands

& wave, which makes the images
almost look like they're flying.
she curls up in the sugar
& says "this is true."

tuck me in

bed bugs are attracted to warmth
which is almost sad
i know that it's just some kind
of bodily impulse
but maybe they're craving
some kind of contact
pressing themselves
to skin at night
in the hopes of feeling warm
spreading out
under sheets
finding leg & arm & finger
stepping with their thin insect limbs
over our full fleshy ones
soft comforter press
the world under the mattress
a kind of matrix of bodies
crossing paths
whispering to each other
will you tuck me in?
will you tuck me in?
not knowing what it means
it's just a phrase passed down
over heard from humans
though i never asked anyone to tuck me in
we slept in a bunk bed &
i'd just pulled the covers over me
making myself a clothe egg case
my brother rolled in the blankets
a cocoon
i would ask him almost each night
after mom or dad left

are you asleep?
are you asleep?
& he would almost always be asleep
so i'd pull the covers tighter
around myself
as if that could keep the room's darkness
from touching me
do they want skin like us?
houses? blood? beds?
somewhere there's a bed bug version
of my brother & i
in little bunk beds
& the older brother
is asking the younger brother
are you asleep?
& the younger brother
repeats *tuck me in tuck me in*
& the bed bugs have bed bug dreams
where we trade places entirely
humans on hands & knees
traversing the great bodies
of the insects
biting with our flimsy teeth
our bodies cold
their bodies so exciting & warm
humans under box springs
holding hands & singing
the bed bugs tell us
to be quiet so we laugh
& scatter ourselves across the insect's belongings
in couches & books & clothing
but despite all of that
we would still not be able
to feel warmth

& we'd return as we must to the bed room
to great bed bug
sleeping there
sprawl ourselves out on his abdomen
as he rests
my brother would be there with me,
already asleep in the folds of blankets
as i lay awake
& pull a small corner of covers
over my head

the capability of filling a glass

when there was no more food
left in the house
there was always a box of powdered milk
perched in the corner of the shelf.

the box had drawings of white flowers
and, sometimes, i'd pull a chair up
to the counter so that i would
be tall enough to reach it.

one hand on the counter,
one hand extending, i'd plucked
the box from it's nesting place.
just to hold it there alone.
barefoot. cold red speckled floor kitchen.

shaking the box i considered
the mechanics of powdered milk,
if, maybe, when i'd pour the stuff
in a glass of water it could do more
than just turn to murky pale milk.

i thought of the flowers on the package
and imagined one of the tall water glasses
filling up with flowers, white flowers
dunked in water, the flowers dissolving
into milk in my mouth.

also maybe, another kind of magic,
the capability of filling a glass
with whatever kind
of food you wanted.

i would stir with a big spoon
and i'd whisper to the opaque water
*Oreos or Milano cookies
or even just spaghetti*
and the powdered milk would choose
for me. the powdered milk
would be motherly like that.

standing there,
i'd shake the box,
listening to the shifting
of dried milk, which sounded
so much like sand. a beach, maybe,
could be built where each time
a wave crash the powdered shore would
make more food; wild snacks
like raspberries and cantaloupe.

after shaking it,
i'd put the box back,
stare at it few seconds, inspecting
those white flowers.

once i tasted a handful
of the powdered milk.
it was bitter and chalky in my mouth.
i washed it down with water
which just made it gunky in my throat.

someone laughing

i fed you with a tablespoon
from the bowl of rainbow sprinkles
because we were hungry & that
was the only thing left in the house.
the crush of their shells
in your teeth; their colorful
exoskeletons gone to sugar powder.
i watched the mashing
the way your chewing made a mess
of the colors,
is there a word for what happens
when you blend together
every color? a collapse of rainbow;
a significant
greenish brown. a stain glaring
down the middle of your tongue.
& the sprinkles scurried,
insects only hatched
when someone somewhere
laughs so hard that they cry.
i want to make you laugh
so hard that you cry
so i clink the spoon
against my teeth,
keys of xylophone,
they play & you recognize
the song. you ask if i
want any sprinkles
if i want a turn eating
& i tell you *no* that
i want to feed you sprinkles
sunup sunset until your

teeth also turn to insects
each a new color not found yet
like butterfly sight
& your scared because i ask
so much of you &
i'm raising the spoon
& the sprinkles are crawling
all up my arm, won't stay still,
want to crawl all over us
& you ask if someone is laughing.
i say *yes there is always
someone laughing.*
you ask *is it me?*
& i'm not sure if you are.
i look again at your teeth,
each becoming a thick colorful beetle
& crawling out of your head.
you know how you never mean
for things to really happen?
that's how i feel, i feel
like i didn't mean to do this
i just wanted to know
what would happen.
i put the spoon in your hand.
there's still a few sprinkles
in the bowl.
i say *feed me, go ahead you
can feed me now.*
you shake your head
& pull the bowl closer
to your chest. no teeth left,
you smile
like a sliced peach
saying,
these are mine.

Self Portrait as Enough

if there is a stone to be
eaten i know it
& i think about the dinosaurs
who ate stones to digest the leafy plants
they swallowed
leaves like feathers of a bird
fossilized in rib cage
my therapist asks me what i think i am
outside of all the things i do
& i want to say *nothing*
by which i mean
i believe i am nothing
outside of what i write
what comes pouring out of me
a stomach full of stones
a green bird
aching with fossil
but instead i tell her
that i like to think
i am kind & that
i read beautiful
people & that i write poetry
enough to make up for the rest
(insert thought about
the purpose a therapist
can serve in a poem)
(insert a thought about
running out of money to see
that therapist who is now
just a line in your poem)
(insert a cup of strawberries
measured perfectly)

(insert a boy who lays on
his stomach by the creek, peels
a layer of moss off a stone before
placing it in his mouth)
(inert a boy not swallowing)
there are good things
that come from heaviness
the way the whole earth might
laugh under the feet of a dinosaur
the way the earth might
laugh when i lay down
& ask again
if i am real
i do not know how many
stones there are to eat
or how i will perfectly fit them
in a measuring cup
but i will find a way
& i do not think i will ever
be a person cured
of all my (insert a list
of sadness here)
but i am placing
a rock in my mouth &
not swallowing

ROBIN GOW is a queer and trans poet and young adult author. They are the author of *Our Lady of Perpetual Degeneracy* (Tolsun Books 2020) and the chapbook *Honeysuckle* (Finishing Line Press 2019). Their first young adult novel, *A Million Quiet Revolutions* is forthcoming with FSG Winter 2022. Gow is also the founder of the trans and queer reading series Gender Reveal Party. They are a managing editor at *The Nasiona*.

www.ingramcontent.com/pod-product-compliance
Lightning Source LLC
Chambersburg PA
CBHW051658040426
42446CB00009B/1194